Sagittarius Horoscope 2024

Angeline A. Rubi

Alina A. Rubi

Published Independently

All rights reserved © 2024.

Astrologer: Alina A. Rubi

Editing: Alina. Rubi and Angeline A. Rubi

rubiediciones29@gmail.com

Who is Sagittarius ? 6

Sagittarius Personality 7

General Horoscope for Sagittarius 9

    Love 11

    Economy 12

    Sagittarius Health 13

    Family 14

    Important Dates 15

    Monthly Horoscopes for Sagittarius 2024 17

January 2024 17

February 2024 18

March 2024 20

Lucky numbers 20

April 2024 21

Lucky numbers 21

May 2024 22

Lucky numbers 22

June 2024 23

July 2024 24

Lucky numbers 25

August 2024 26

September 2024 27

Lucky numbers 27

October 2024 28

Lucky numbers 28

November 2024 29

Lucky numbers 29

December 2024 30

Lucky numbers 30

The Tarot Cards, an Enigmatic and Psychological World. 31

    Wheel of Fortune Tarot Card for Sagittarius 2024 34

Runes of the Year 2024 36

Thurisaz, Rune of Sagittarius 2024 37

Lucky Colors 39

Sagittarius 41

Lucky Charms 42

Lucky Quartz 45

Lucky Charm for Sagittarius 48

Sagittarius and Zodiac Sign Compatibility 49

Sagittarius 49

Sagittarius and Vocation 60

Best Professions 60

Signs not to do business with 61

Signs to be associated with 61

Money Rituals 61

Best Countries and Cities to Live In 70

Incense and Essential Oils for Money 71

Plants for Money 71

Quartz for Money 71

Money Charms 72

Pentacles to Thrive 72

Affirmations to Receive Money 74

Vacations 75

Who is your soul mate according to your zodiac sign? 79

Madness and Zodiac Signs 83

The psychology behind the lottery 87

The best gifts for zodiac signs 90

The zodiac signs and their fears. 93

Moon in Sagittarius 96

The importance of the Ascendant Sign 98

Ascendant in Sagittarius 103

Aries - Sagittarius Ascendant 103

Taurus - Sagittarius Ascendant 104

Gemini - Sagittarius Ascendant 105

Cancer - Sagittarius Ascendant 106

Leo - Sagittarius Ascendant 106

Virgo - Sagittarius Ascendant 107

Libra - Sagittarius Ascendant 108

Scorpio - Sagittarius Ascendant 108

Sagittarius - Sagittarius Ascendant 109

Capricorn - Sagittarius Ascendant 110

Aquarius - Sagittarius Ascendant 110

Pisces - Sagittarius Ascendant 111

Saturn in Pisces, one of the most important astrological events. 112

How will it affect the Sagittarius Sign? 120

Bibliography 126

About the Authors 127

Who is Sagittarius?

Dates: November 23 - December 21

Day: Thursday

Color: purple blue, green and white

Element: fire

Compatibility: Libra, Gemini, Leo, and Aries

Symbol:

Mode: mutable

Polarity: male

Ruling Planet: Jupiter

House: 9

Metal: Tin

Quartz: Turquoise and Topaz

Constellation: Sagittarius

Sagittarius Personality

Sagittarius is one of the most positive signs of the zodiac. They are versatile and love adventure and the unknown. They are open-minded to innovative ideas and experiences and maintain an optimistic attitude even when the going gets tough.

They are open and cheerful people who transmit positive energy to the people around them. They have a religious and spiritual nature and high morals.

Sagittarius is a sign that loves to discover, travel abroad, explore, adventure, risk, try their luck, broaden their knowledge, and enjoys their social life. Sagittarius takes life with humor, with philosophy.

They are attracted to risky sports and those that can be practiced alone because of their strong self-confidence, travel that allows them to meet cultures and religions other than their own, nature, knowledge, religion, philosophy, laws, justice, and social norms.

If they enjoy a stable and balanced relationship, Sagittarians show their best side and will be excellent fathers and husbands, transmitting moral and ethical values to their children, besides showing their jovial, cheerful, and enthusiastic side among their own. They are very enthusiastic and carpe diem could be their motto in life since they are so enthusiastic that they do not want to waste any second of their days. They are good friends, noble, loyal, and sincere. Precisely this sincerity can turn against them and create conflicts with people who think differently from them.

They are empathetic, good counselors, they are positive, they tend to simplify things, they see the good side of everything and therefore tend to self-deception. They do not like routine, they are dynamic, adaptable, honest, and naive. Their audacity makes them like nature, travel, adventure.

A Sagittarius is a spiritual, philosophical, and deep soul. One of the things that is most appealing about Sagittarians is their ability to see the bigger picture, and to be able to give advice for their friends' problems. Sagittarians attract wealth or generate it. They have the ideas, energy, and talent to make their vision a reality. However, wealth alone is not enough.

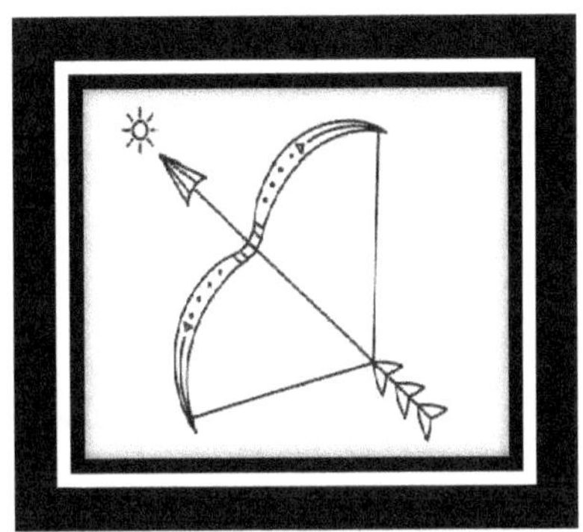

General Horoscope for Sagittarius

This will be a promising year for Sagittarius. Your personal and professional life will be good, although they will have their share of challenges and responsibilities.

You will have to make some important decisions, therefore, you should rely on the advice of your friends and loved ones.

This is a period that will take you out of your routine and encourage you to pursue your life's ambitions. This will be a year that will give you a sense of fulfillment.

This is a lucky year for Sagittarius, but hard work and commitment would be the key to being able to succeed. Do not be shortsighted, learn to look at the big picture. All your moves should be made wisely.

Beginning May 25, Jupiter, your ruler, transits into Gemini. This will help you get closer to your destiny.

During periods of Mercury Retrograde you are likely to want to plan new beginnings and focus on second chances.

During New Moon periods you may be presented with unique opportunities, so you must be very smart with your decisions and have faith in yourself.

During full Moon periods your emotions will be at their peak, you should pay more attention to your desires and needs.

Sagittarius' health will be average for this year. You should be alert and concerned about your general well-being. You will have stages of high stress and anxiety that will affect your health. Unhealthy habits could interfere with your heart health.

Be wary of addictions. Get enough rest and rely more on home-cooked meals than fast food.

The year is favorable for your family life, you will have prosperity and happiness in your home. However, the health of your children may cause you to worry.

Those who wish to have a baby will be able to conceive during the last months of 2024.

Love will blossom, but you must try to resolve any differences that exist in your relationship.

Love

This year you will pay extra attention to your love relationships, as any existing problems may worsen. You must work to remove blockages in love.

During Eclipse periods you can reconnect with old loves. Eclipses can remind you to be cheerful, have fun and let love into your life if you are single.

Full Moon periods will bring you closer to those with whom you have strong ties and with whom you feel a spiritual connection, but you will stay away from toxic people.

Jupiter after May 25 and for the rest of 2024 will bring energy to your relationships. You will have the opportunity to meet many important people and from these new connections a love may arise.

If you are in a relationship, you may decide to commit.

During new Moon periods you will be open to commitment, and to emotional and physical bonds with others. Sentimentality, sensuality, passion, and lots of fun await you.

Economy

Uranus continues to bring changes to your work life, but Jupiter gives you opportunities to make the changes you desire.

You will have new opportunities for projects, or a completely new job that will excite you.

Keep an eye on new Moon periods because it is during them that new opportunities will appear for you to prosper.

You will be more productive, efficient, and organized, and any projects you participate in will bear a lot of fruit, meaning a lot of money, after August.

During Full Moon periods you will feel emotionally connected to your work or profession. During these periods you will approach the end of important stages for you financially.

You must have financial plans and invest wisely. Do not get carried away with ordinary investment options because you can lose your capital. Jupiter and Saturn favor your long-term investment plans. In general, this is a year in which you will not feel any fiscal crisis.

Sagittarius Health

As you are such an active sign, you run the risk of not realizing how chronic fatigue and stress accumulate. It is advisable that you dedicate time to relaxation. Massages, chatting with friends, and walking along the beach will improve your mood and your appetite.

A healthy diet is recommended, try to consume enough foods rich in vitamins. Due to deficiency of certain vitamins, you may experience skin problems.

You should avoid nervous tensions and not take on so many responsibilities at once. A vacation by the sea would not only be exciting but will have a beneficial effect on your physical and mental well-being.

Some Sagittarians will have several dental appointments, and others will sadly say goodbye to their favorite foods. You must go on a diet.

Any effort will not be in vain. Moderation and a focus on your health will become sources of optimism.

Family

There may be some nebulous issues in your home, but these events will strengthen your emotional intuition.

Some old problems related to your home and family will have to be eliminated. This may mean several periods of uncertainty, instability, or lack of family connection.

You may move to another location, or buy property, expand the family, or take on large family responsibilities. New Moon periods are the ones that can bring these opportunities.

Be incredibly careful during Lunar Eclipses as this strong energy can amplify any family problems. The smart thing to do would be to try to make things better before the Eclipse.

Important Dates

01/ 02- Mercury transits direct in Sagittarius.

You will be able to communicate more fluently, your thoughts will focus more easily on the future.

05/23- Full Moon in Sagittarius.

You will have the opportunity to let go of ways of thinking that limit your growth. It is the perfect time to broaden your perspective and feel more confident. This Full Moon marks the end of emotional attachments that are uncoordinated with your energy. A chapter in your life related to financial matters closes. You must find balance in your daily routines.

10/17- Venus transits Sagittarius.

It is the time to conquer as your aura will be magnetic. Seriousness will not be part of your romantic plans and you will have the opportunity to try new things.

11/ 02- Mercury transits Sagittarius.

You will have a clearer understanding of people's motivations and actions.

11/21- Sun enters Sagittarius.

11/ 26- Mercury Retrograde in Sagittarius.

Avoid signing agreements. Reflect on your past, learn to ask for forgiveness and be flexible with your schedule. Plan everything in advance. Do not make important decisions.

12/ 01- New Moon in Sagittarius.

Analyze your personal relationships, take things calmly and free yourself from stress. Eliminate routine, plan new things with effort and dedication. Set solid goals.

12/ 06- Sun conjunct Mercury in Sagittarius.

Perfect day for you to communicate your ideas with clarity and confidence.

12/15- Mercury direct in Sagittarius.

You will be able to communicate more fluently, your thoughts will focus more easily on the future.

Monthly Horoscopes for Sagittarius 2024

January 2024

This month you will receive some extra money, do not waste it. It is always healthy to have an emergency plan in case things go wrong.

It is a month where you should be more present in the lives of the people you love, not that you spend every day with them, but if you take the time to share some days within the month.

In the middle of the month, you will feel very enthusiastic, you should channel that enthusiasm by decorating your home.

You will not be able to reach an agreement with someone at work and unfortunately this situation will drag on for several weeks. Remember that communication is an especially important part of this discussion.

You may wonder if you should say yes to a request made by a person you had not noticed. You should do it because this person will play a special role in your life, and it will mean a singular and necessary story. One of true love.

You are giving up money by not giving up your arm in an unimportant dispute.

Lucky numbers

12-19 -21 -33-36

February 2024

Organize your schedule better so that the necessary sleep time is not affected. Your dreams will only come to guide you if you give them the necessary time and space.

Gifts are an essential part of romance, but those gifts are no substitute for presence and care, quality time and love itself.

If you are alone, do not let it be envy that brings you closer to that person, it was the partner of someone who has unresolved issues with you, but love cannot be revenge.

You will be offered a particularly good deal by someone who is confident that you will be able to complete it, show your appreciation for being considered for this proposal and try.

Do not forget that you must keep abreast of all the modern technologies and novel studies that have come out in the profession you are in.

Do not be afraid to love again, the person who has come into your life is making you see things in a unique way, but you are afraid to give yourself because of bad experiences you lived, trust more in life.

Lucky numbers

4 - 17 - 20 - 33 - 35

March 2024

This month you will have to make a weighty decision in love, since a person you like very much does not feel the same for you. You should pay attention because there is someone else in your life who has all his attention on you and you have not wanted to give him entrance to your heart, you should analyze well what you want.

You should not fall into erratic behavior just because some of your friends do it, it is not fair to the people who love you. If you are in a moment of weakness of character and want to try things you should not, you should first think about the consequences it will have for your family and for your future.

A mistake you made in the past will come back to haunt you, so you may have to apologize or pay something you owe.

At the end of the month the speed of your thinking accelerates, you will realize that what used to take you hours to process will be done in a few minutes. With this mental predisposition you can achieve many things.

***Lucky numbers**
2 - 10 - 18 - 19 - 23*

April 2024

This month you should not be postponing everything you want to do because of what you have an obligation to do. The time has come to take charge of your life and begin to organize your priorities, which should always include the time to do the things you enjoy.

You cannot keep an eye on everyone's life. You must let those around you know that they must make decisions for themselves, as you are not always going to be there to help them.

Someone has been taking advantage of your kindness, you have thought about it, but you have not wanted to accept the truth, it is time to do it, because you can no longer accept that deal where you are not receiving anything in return for your efforts.

Your mind is in a period of immense creativity. You possess a constant thirst for information. Quench your thirst by taking an advanced training course that will help you become better at your profession.

There are people who want to damage your partner's reputation by spreading rumors. You should listen carefully and protect yourself from such people.

Lucky numbers
2 - 8 - 26 - 30 - 33

May 2024

This is a perfect month to negotiate and close deals. Money will come to you in mysterious ways.

Remember that excess is an enemy. Organization will be key this month along with patience and the ability to turn negatives into positives.

You must strive to create balance between home, family, friends, and your financial future.

In the name of love, you must restrain your flirting. Align your heart and desires.

Always try to be on time for work, complete all your tasks and be very responsible.

If you are single, you will have the perfect opportunity to find a new love. If you have a stable relationship, it is time to strengthen those sentimental ties, and if the relationship is long distance, do not forget to show how much you care about your partner.

There may be some discomfort due to liver problems, keep control, limit alcohol, and follow a good diet to relieve your body.

Lucky numbers
5 - 12 - 16 - 22 - 27

June 2024

You are wasting your time and talent; you should not give up because your efforts will be rewarded. Plan your economy if you do not want to have unpleasant surprises. You must take all decisions with great courage.

You have been going through a lot of stress lately and the consequences are starting to emerge. You have had to put up with a lot, but the problems are starting to resolve themselves and it is time for you to take it easy.

Do not underestimate some changes, some of them are positive, but others may not be as favorable as they seem at first glance. Do not rush and analyze the alternatives and prospects of each option.

You are likely to argue with a friend and end up withdrawing your confidence in him. This whole situation is due to nervousness about economic circumstances that should not be allowed to influence you negatively.

Try to internalize opportunities as you are in for a surprise. Walk at your own pace, something big is coming.

Lucky numbers

14 - 17 - 24 - 29 – 30

July 2024

This month remember that your heart and your head should not be in conflict. You may change your place of work this month, do not despair.

You will have the courage to face the problem of an outstanding debt, as well as the ability to negotiate the type of payment plan you can afford.

After the 14th there will be an argument with your partner, he/she will say hurtful things to you. It is up to you to decide whether to continue next to someone capable of hurting you.

In your workplace there are people who do not have your skills and knowledge, but who occupy more important and better paid positions than yours. You feel that your preparation and knowledge are not recognized, and you feel undervalued. All this happens because you do not know how to demand what is rightfully yours. You must fight for what you want and avoid giving in easily.

You should focus on taking a direction on what you want or do not want to do in the future, do not be afraid.

Lucky numbers
6 - 8 - 22 - 25 - 35

August 2024

You do not have the patience required to cultivate long-term relationships. You always want immediate results, which can get in the way of your growth.

You will attend a group party where you and that special someone will leave early to spend some time for an intimate conversation.

To understand the ways of love you must ask your friends for advice. If you want to have a partner, you must take care of it.

A perfect month for those who want to buy a house, at least you must start saving to be able to do so.

There is a person who has a lot of interest in you but is losing it seeing the coldness you behave.

You need to control your expenses; you will go over your budget and that will affect you in a way you do not expect.

Lucky numbers

5 - 12 - 21 - 22 - 23

September 2024

This month does not indicate that there will be major changes in your love life. Those in a stable relationship will not experience major changes, and singles are not likely to find their soul mate either.

Whoever you work for may be undergoing major changes and you may even be offered the chance to work abroad or to go on work-related trips.

You will be prone to pay less attention to your health, it is important that you try not to fall into this tendency. A good diet, exercise and a healthy lifestyle will fill you with vitality. You should avoid excesses; you could end up stressed or anxious.

Possibilities for romances outside of your marriage may arise, but this does not mean that you will take advantage of them.

Anyway, your relationship as a couple is being evaluated, it is important that, when faced with small misunderstandings, you do not withdraw thinking that everything is solved by itself, try to be initiative-taking to solve it by talking and listening.

***Lucky numbers**
4 - 8 - 12 - 13 - 22*

October 2024

This month your work and profession will continue with its inertia. You will think about taking a vacation, for that reason you will not have to work a lot and you will not have to make important decisions.

You will do well financially anyway, but things will evolve slowly. It is not the month for big investments, you should buy the basics for your life without excessive expenses.

You will enjoy exercising and going out at night with your friends.

In love you will do well. If you have a partner, the relationship will progress smoothly. If you are single, it could be a month in which you will be phenomenally successful with a different sex, so you could have several sporadic relationships. The issue is that you are not clear whether you want to commit or not. Even if you meet someone special, you will let him or her slip away. Your desire to advance and your ambition will make you focused on work at the end of the month, because you want to succeed. Your home will be incredibly quiet, but the challenge of the month is to combine your work with your family.

Lucky numbers

4 - 8 - 12 - 13 - 22

November 2024

This month fatigue and stress will weaken you; you must stay as strong as possible. Sleep well, rest, take vitamins, do whatever is necessary so that it does not affect you too much.

If you are in a relationship, you will feel good, but you will begin to question whether that relationship is really what you need. This will cause you to be focused on your thoughts. If you are alone, it is not a month to start a stable relationship. Not because you will not find interesting people, but because you do not know well what you want.

Economically it is a good period and money will come in easily. Good period to invest in the long term, you should think about your future.

You should take advantage and start planning a vacation, to rest and recharge your batteries. You will need to be in shape for the coming year 2025.

Take care of yourself, it is no use killing yourself doing exercises only to get injured and must be inactive for a while.

Lucky numbers
11 - 12 - 13 - 17 - 25

December 2024

If you have a partner, you will have a good calm, but you will feel that your partner is a little uncoordinated. This means that you are not coordinated, but you should not worry, because it is not your fault, it is she who does not know what she wants. If you are single, it is a good month to meet people. Do not rush into things, take your time to get to know this person well and do not make a mistake.

Money will come to you from various sources, which will fill your bank account to overflowing. If you have investments, they will give you profits. You will feel lucky, and you will be able to treat yourself to some luxuries and whims. People will see you as a millionaire. It is a fantastic month for your economy.

Your home will be particularly good, as you will do so well with money, you will be able to give them gifts. You will feel loved, and you will notice their unconditional support.

You will have energy to do whatever you want. You will have fun with yourself. Your image will be attractive, and you will feel satisfied. Avoid accidents.

Lucky numbers
2 - 7 - 17 - 25 - 36

The Tarot Cards, an Enigmatic and Psychological World.

The word Tarot means "royal road", it is a millenary practice, it is not known exactly who invented card games in general, nor the Tarot in particular; there are the most dissimilar hypotheses in this sense.

Some say that it arose in Atlantis or Egypt, but others believe that tarots came from China or India, from the ancient land of the gypsies, or that they arrived in Europe through the Cathars. The fact is that tarot cards distill astrological, alchemical, esoteric, and religious symbolism, both Christian and pagan.

Until recently, if you mentioned the word 'tarot' to some people, it was common for them to imagine a gypsy sitting in front of a crystal ball in a room surrounded by mysticism, or to think of black magic or witchcraft, but nowadays this has changed.

This ancient technique has been adapting to the modern times, it has joined technology and many young people feel a deep interest in it.

Young people have isolated themselves from religion because they believe that they will not find the solution to what they need there, they realized the duality of this, something that does not happen with spirituality. All over the social networks you find accounts dedicated to the study and tarot readings, since everything related to esotericism is fashionable, in fact, some hierarchical decisions are made considering the tarot or astrology.

What is remarkable is that the predictions that are usually related to tarot are not the most sought after, the ones related to self-knowledge and spiritual counseling are the most requested.

The tarot is an oracle, through its drawings and colors, we stimulate our psychic sphere, the innermost part that goes beyond the natural. Many people turn to the tarot as a spiritual or psychological guide because we live in uncertain times, and this pushes us to seek answers in spirituality.

It is such a powerful tool that tells you concretely what is going on in your subconscious so that you can perceive it through the lens of a new wisdom.

Carl Gustav Jung, the famed psychologist, used the symbols of tarot cards in his psychological studies.

He created the theory of archetypes, where he discovered an extensive sum of images that help in analytical psychology.

The use of drawings and symbols to appeal to a deeper understanding is frequently used in psychoanalysis. These allegories are part of us, corresponding to symbols of our subconscious and our mind.

Our unconscious has dark areas, and when we use visual techniques, we can reach various parts of it and reveal elements of our personality that we do not know. When you can decode these messages through the pictorial language of tarot, you can choose what decisions to make in life to create the destiny you really want.

The tarot with its symbols teaches us that a different universe exists, especially nowadays where everything is so chaotic, and a logical explanation is sought for everything.

Wheel of Fortune Tarot Card for Sagittarius 2024

Favorable change, luck, new conditions, and improvements.

Success and evolution thanks to your creativity, luck in games of chance, balance between opposing forces. This card represents the principle of polarity that leads us to face changes with courage.

It symbolizes the cycles of life and speaks of new beginnings, transformations governed by destiny and, therefore, out of your control.

The desire for adventure, spontaneity, and good humor.

It portends victories and success. However, you must remember that nothing comes on a silver platter.

Even if success comes knocking at your door, you must continue to strive for it.

It means a well-deserved victory.

It symbolizes hard work and dedication, indicating that success will not come easy, you must earn it.

You must take charge of your destiny and prepare to take advantage of the opportunities that this year 2024 will give you.

Runes of the Year 2024

Runes are a set of symbols that form an alphabet. "Rune" means secret and symbolizes the noise of one stone colliding with another. Runes are an ancient visionary and magical method.

Runes do not serve for exact predictions, but they do serve to guide you about a future event, a subject, or a decision.

The runes have a specific meaning for the person who wants it, but also some message related to the adversities that arise in life.

Thurisaz, Rune of Sagittarius 2024

This is the year to make decisions. However, remember that a hasty decision causes serious mistakes. Therefore, avoid impulsive acts, try not to do anything that exceeds your capabilities. In other words, think well before you act.

There are always external factors beyond your control, so you must be tolerant.

You still have a long way to go, you should wait and, before taking the first step, analyze the situation, the past, your mistakes and successes. Then when the time comes you will be able to make the right decision.

Do not act until conditions are favorable.

The work you must do is not only external, but you must also calmly review your heart and soul. Analyze how you have arrived now and visualize the achievements and challenges before acting.

Thurisaz warns you that what you are really facing is the reflection of what is hidden in your subconscious.

The energy of the conflict you are going through is neutral, for that reason you must accept the dynamics involved.

This rune announces that you are protected and that you have the power to face any obstacle.

Lucky Colors

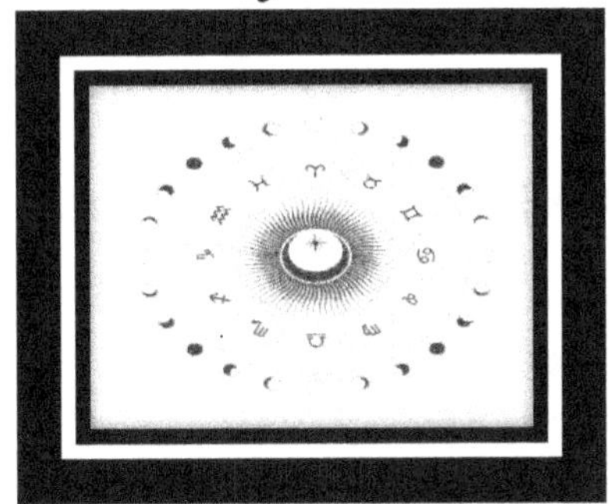

Colors affect us psychologically; they influence our appreciation of things, opinion about something or someone, and can be used to influence our decisions.

Traditions to welcome the new year vary from country to country, and on the night of December 31 we take stock of all the positive and negative things we experienced in the year that is leaving. We start thinking about what to do to transform our luck in the new year ahead.

There are several ways to attract positive energies towards us when we receive the new year, and one of them is to wear or wear accessories of a specific color that attracts what we wish for the year that is about to begin.

Colors have energetic charges that influence our lives, so it is always advisable to receive the year dressed in a color that attracts the energies of what we want to achieve.

For that there are colors that vibrate positively with each zodiac sign, so the recommendation is that you wear the clothes with the hue that will make you attract prosperity, health, and love in 2024. (These colors can also be used during the rest of the year for important occasions, or to enhance your days).

Remember that, although the most common is to wear red underwear for passion, pink for love and yellow or gold for abundance, it is never too much to include in our attire the color that most benefits our zodiac sign.

Sagittarius

Orange

The key words for orange are *energy, joy, happiness, and creativity.*

Orange is a cheerful color that helps to release negative emotions. Using it will make you feel confident, and sympathetic to other people's shortcomings.

Orange is a color that stimulates the mind, renews illusions and is antidepressant.

Orange is widely used in Buddhism, as it is associated with the sacral chakra, and is related to sexuality, creativity, and passion. This chakra is associated with the water element and helps to balance emotions and increase vital energies.

Lucky Charms

Who does not own a lucky ring, a chain that never comes off, or an object that they would not give away for anything in the world? We all attribute a special power to certain items that belong to us and that distinctive character that they assume for us makes them magical objects.

For a talisman to act and influence circumstances, its bearer must have faith in it, and this will transform it into an immense object, able to accomplish everything that is asked of it.

Usually, an amulet is any object that propitiates good as a preventive measure against evil, harm, disease, and witchcraft.

Amulets for good luck can help you to have a year 2024 full of blessings in your home, work, with your family, attract money and health. For the amulets to work properly you should not lend them to anyone else, and you should always have them at hand.

Amulets have existed in all cultures and are made from elements of nature that serve as catalysts of energies that help create human desires.

The amulet is assigned the power to ward off evils, spells, diseases, disasters or to counteract evil wishes cast through the eyes of others.

Amulet for Sagittarius

Horse

Horses are considered symbols of wealth. In ancient times horses were given as gifts to emperors and kings because they are symbols of triumph and success.

Horses signify power, strength, and courage. They are a symbol of speed, courage, and perseverance.

They are associated with the Fire element and represent fame, freedom and achievement of goals that require your energetic strength.

You can put ornaments with the figure of a horse, or several in the living room, study, office or if you work at home place it on your desk. As it is considered an amulet to attract success and good luck it must be near you.

Lucky Quartz

We are all attracted to diamonds, rubies, emeralds and sapphires, obviously precious stones. Semi-precious stones such as carnelian, tiger's eye, white quartz, and lapis lazuli are also highly prized as they have been used as ornaments and symbols of power for thousands of years.

What many do not know is that they were valued for more than their beauty: each had a sacred significance, and their healing properties were as important as their ornamental value.

Crystals still have the same properties in our days, most people are familiar with the most popular ones such as amethyst, malachite and obsidian, but nowadays there are new crystals such as larimar, petalite and phenacite that have become known.

A crystal is a solid body with a geometrically regular shape, crystals were formed when the earth was created and have continued to metamorphose as the planet has changed, crystals are the DNA of the earth, they are miniature stores that contain the development of our planet over millions of years.

Some have been bent to extraordinary pressures and others grew in chambers buried deep underground, others dripped into being. Whatever form they take, their crystalline structure can absorb, conserve, focus and emit energy.

At the heart of the crystal is the atom, its electrons, and protons. The atom is dynamic and is composed of a series of particles that rotate around the center in constant motion, so that, although the crystal may seem motionless, it is a living molecular mass that vibrates at a certain frequency, and this is what gives energy to the crystal.

Gems used to be a royal and priestly prerogative, the priests of Judaism wore a plaque on their chest full of precious stones which was much more than an emblem to designate their function, as it transferred power to the wearer.

Men have worn stones since the stone age as they had a protective function guarding their wearers from various evils. Today's crystals have the same power, and we can select our jewelry not only according to their external attractiveness, having them near us can boost our energy (orange carnelian), clean the space around us (amber) or attract wealth (citrine).

Certain crystals such as smoky quartz and black tourmaline can absorb negativity, emitting a pure and clean energy.

Wearing a black tourmaline around the neck protects from electromagnetic emanations including that of cell phones, a citrine will not only attract wealth, but will also help you keep it, place it in the wealthy part of your home (the back left most away from the front door).

If you are looking for love, crystals can help you, place a rose quartz in the relationship corner of your house (the back right corner furthest away from the front door) its effect is so powerful that you may want to add an amethyst to offset the attraction.

You can also use rhodochrosite, love will come your way.

Crystals can heal and give balance, some crystals contain minerals known for their therapeutic properties, malachite has a high concentration of copper, wearing a malachite bracelet allows the body to absorb minimal amounts of copper.

Lapis lazuli relieves migraine, but if the headache is caused by stress, amethyst, amber or turquoise placed above the eyebrows will relieve it.

Quartz and minerals are jewels of mother earth, give yourself the opportunity, and connect with the magic they give off.

Lucky Charm for Sagittarius

Agate

A quartz with great energetic power. It helps to increase self-esteem and transforms negative energies into positive ones.

It helps emotional, mental, and physical stability. It is good for migraines, relieves all kinds of physical ailments, such as muscle, joint and bone pain.

It is known as the stone of confidence. It will bring you wealth and abundance in all areas of your life.

It helps to develop creativity and security. It is also assigned powers to evade curses.

If you place it under your pillow, you will not have problems to sleep, you will avoid insomnia, stress at night, or anxieties.

It will give you a calculating mentality.

It acts as an amulet so that things go well, and you obtain prosperity in a brief period.

To take advantage of the protective qualities of this quartz you should always have it with you.

Sagittarius and Zodiac Sign Compatibility

Sagittarius

Sagittarius is a sign that is eternally collecting knowledge. You can find him crossing the seas and delving into every nook and cranny of the universe on his travels in his quest for thrills.

When it comes to love, every day and hour is an adventure for this active fire sign. Jupiter, the planet of abundance is the ruler of Sagittarius, luck follows this sign wherever it goes, and as an astrological centaur, Sagittarius desires mental, philosophical, and spiritual development, and of course lots of fun.

Sagittarius can turn anything, even the earthliest activity, into a fascinating feat. Everyone has a story, and since Sagittarius is a superb speaker, he can share these memories with friends, family, and outsiders alike in ways that inspire and enlighten anywhere. As well as eliciting infectious laughter from your audience.

As this fire sign is attractive, it is always surrounded by eager onlookers, in other words, this sign is the famous child of the zodiac. As a mutable sign, Sagittarius is also adaptable, in fact, it has a deep-rooted desire for repeated change. Sagittarius loves to acquire new ethics, ideologies, and logics, change perspectives and, most importantly, travel the world.

The zodiac hiker has a wandering quality and can get fickle if he or she lingers in one place for too long, so it is critical that this sign has the freedom to explore. Not everyone can keep up with Sagittarius' ever-shifting restlessness, so when it comes to passion, this fire sign is known to win hearts.

Sagittarius is also the clown of the zodiac, always telling a story or a joke, so that every conversation is imbued with witticisms, and considerable sincerity. Although they have no opponent, Sagittarius must remember to be careful with their sharp tongue and satirical remarks. Occasionally, their energy goes over the edge, making them look presumptuous or even contemptible.

Sagittarius' mutable quality makes him a bit rough when it comes to decisions such as making a commitment in a relationship. Having so many possibilities, he suffers from choosing the right relationship as he likes to keep his options open.

To avoid feeling overshadowed, you must be honest with this sign, talk to him, be firm, and everything will be fine because if there is something that Sagittarius appreciates is sincerity.

With his unchanging adventurous spirit, dating Sagittarius is like flying in a balloon, or jumping out of a parachute in severe weather, because he likes to live on the edge, where there is a greater chance of discovering something new.

When it comes to relationships things get dicey with Sagittarius, as he may be encouraged to pursue high-risk relationships. It is not easy to get Sagittarius' attention the Centaur does not stay in one place long enough to maintain motivation. Therefore, if you are trying to win over a Sagittarius, you will have to keep this dynamic sign on their toes - do not be afraid to show off the more energetic aspects of your personality.

Sagittarius is attracted to you standing up for yourself, so be sure to keep your communication style friendly. Lively and free-spirited, the centaur tends to have a carefree aspect when it comes to sexuality, and their physical relationships can range from accidental to committed, and being a natural archeologist, sex is always an event for this fiery sign.

Sagittarius sees intimacy as an occasion for self-discovery and intellectual recreation, so when it comes to sex, they tend to be serious thrill seekers. When Sagittarius decides to commit things do not change you have to try to maintain an adventurous lifestyle 24/7.

Serious relationships are about sharing weaknesses, creating a method of support, and addressing realities together, but if your schedule cannot withstand

Sagittarius' proposed program, try to make every day a success.

Consider exploring alternative wellness practices with your Centaur partner; he will love developing his spiritual boundaries with you by his side. When it comes to adventure, Sagittarius is simply looking for a fun companion; he wants to be with someone who will challenge him to expand his horizons. But never forget that even in a relationship, Sagittarius hates boundaries, so if you find yourself in a relationship with this sign, make sure you have your dock ready. You will not know what is coming, but it is sure to be an unforgiving ride.

Boundaries are not a sad thing; in fact, they provide a solid framework for the relationship. When you are in a relationship with Sagittarius, try to create things from the beginning that clarify the dos and don'ts of a relationship. If you want your Sagittarius to text you every night, you should tell him or her from the beginning, because it will be easier for Sagittarius to understand the relationship if the rules are clear. Sagittarius is always looking for new thrills, his freedom must be respected to keep any long-term relationship healthy, let him know that you are eager to participate in his occupations, but allow him to make the decision for himself and avoid making him feel guilty if he decides to do it on his own.

Sagittarius is very sincere, so when he initiates a breakup, the terms are simple, if he says it is over, it is over, with him there is no going back. Being a bohemian, he finds it easy to pack up and leave when things do not work out. In fact, Sagittarius can often move on as if a relationship never existed in the first place.

Sagittarius and Aries *are a relationship full of energy. Sagittarius has an infectious vitality, is fun, and curious. Hardly anyone can walk in step with a Sagittarius, Aries, however, admires and is inspired by this active sign. Aries' own rousing energy is honed by Sagittarius' fire, and within the relationship, both are motivated to explore their inherent curiosities. While this relationship may be forever, they must be careful. This couple is a fuel truck, as both signs can be extremely explosive. Each must make the commitment to give the other plenty of space to relax after a fight.*

Sagittarius and Taurus *have needs that are quite opposite. Taurus requires to keep its comfort zone intact, with no threats to its security, while Sagittarius needs the excitement and purity of exploration. Taurus links success to things, while Sagittarius links its achievements to adventure. Taurus is boastful of its firm thoughts, while Sagittarius values the power to change its way of thinking. Although these two signs* *exist in different parallel universes, they can come together in a relationship. If they can find a way to appreciate their opposing viewpoints, this relationship offers a powerful balance that inspires both signs.*

Sagittarius and Gemini *are opposite signs. Not all opposite signs are compatible, but this union is one of the most complete associations that exist in astrology. Sagittarius has to do with the general landscape. Gemini, on the other hand, is prompted by what exists on a more concrete level. This air sign explores all the minute details, filling in the gaps of Sagittarius. When partnered, these two signs inspire each other in what makes them curious.*

Sagittarius and Cancer, it *is a difficult relationship, but when it comes to matters of the heart, nothing is impossible. When this relationship is at its best, Sagittarius will be fascinated to share his stories with Cancer, who is an excellent listener. However, these two signs exist in different spaces. Cancer requires a home to feel secure, while Sagittarius' happiness depends on their independence to wander. Honest communication is always key in love, if these signs are brave, they can move forward together and make it happen.*

Sagittarius and Leo *are synonymous with passion and love. Sagittarius is bewitched by the dramatic Leo, and Leo is totally charmed by the fiery Sagittarius. In isolation, these signs have two of the zodiac's greatest natures, so when they reach their vortex, the dynamic is enthusiastic, creative, and full of vitality. Simply put, it just makes sense. However, these highly compatible fire signs will quickly realize that there is no such thing as a perfect relationship. The self-centered Leo needs the security and honesty of a dependable partner, and Sagittarius often cannot offer those things. It is nothing personal, simply no relationship will replace Sagittarius' freedom. This, of course, is difficult for Leo to accept, so this couple can often get entangled in conflict.*

Sagittarius and Virgo *are one of the least likely couples to survive. Virgo labels and organizes everything, and Sagittarius hates to feel labeled. Since Sagittarius is always chasing his arrow, he has a reputation for being unreliable. Virgo will logically have a lot of trouble staying current with his ever-uncertain itinerary, so when engaged, the centaur must go the extra mile and treat his Virgo well. Virgo is never one to invent an affair, but when the right occasion comes along, he is curious. Virgo is sober and does not get carried away by his desires. Sagittarius likes to learn. For the two of them to get* *the most out of this relationship, Virgo should stop examining everything in detail and live in the moment; and Sagittarius should be very patient. If you both agree, your sex life will be very enjoyable.*

In this relationship tension will be present, this couple must find common ground through shared interests and explore the opportunity to create a language that is uniquely theirs.

Sagittarius and Libra *often start out as friends, both signs are extremely intellectual, so they connect on a mental level. Of course, sexual attraction develops quickly. Libra is ruled by Venus, while Sagittarius is ruled by Jupiter, the two planets known as benefits, this union is extremely benevolent. Everything is grander than life with these two signs, even fights. Sagittarius is sometimes disillusioned by Libra's seductive nature, and Libra can easily become annoyed with Sagittarius' conclusive attitude. But even in the worst-case scenario, Sagittarius and Libra really get along. If Libra expresses from the heart, and Sagittarius maintains patience, their romantic glow will continue to burn brightly for the rest of their lives, even after they part ways. Libra is more sentimental than Sagittarius, but there is a lot of sexual compatibility between them. The understanding Libra seeks to satisfy and is prone to view sexuality as an art. Both must create the proper setting for love.*

Sagittarius and Scorpio *are quite different in several respects, although both are enthusiastic people. Scorpio's passion is driven by emotions, while Sagittarius' passion is fueled by curiosity. When they come together, these passions create a dynamic energy focused on enjoying life to the fullest. Sex can help them, but for them to succeed, the relationship requires extreme commitment. Scorpio and Sagittarius may have something special, but they must put in a lot of effort.*

Sagittarius and Sagittarius, *when they line up their bows, their arrows and get on their horses they travel far. This couple is great, together they travel, learn and, most importantly, have fun. Neither takes life too seriously, which can make it difficult for them to form a lasting, committed relationship. Since neither Centaur would dare confine the other, it takes a long time for the Sagittarius-Sagittarius pairing to become official. But really, that is the way these archers like it, and this couple will always be more committed to their individual novelties, than to the couple.*

Sagittarius and Capricorn, *when they come together from the beginning, feel a tension that is difficult to overcome. Sagittarius is ruled by Jupiter, while*

Capricorn is ruled by Saturn, the two planets that are considered ringleaders in astrology. Jupiter has to do with the spreading of boundaries, while Saturn is linked to limitation. Similarly, this relationship can be perceived as a discrepancy. However, through thoughtful exchange, and reciprocal understanding, this relationship can be successful. It is likely that Sagittarius will never understand why Capricorn is always so cautious, and Capricorn is upset by Sagittarius' rigid optimism. Either way, this connection is based on mutual respect, and if the two of you trust and support each other, the relationship has the potential to sail through all problems.

***Sagittarius and Aquarius** have substantial chemistry. Both signs are independent, and each values the other's unique approach to life. Although Sagittarius is more flexible than Aquarius, both signs know that life exists outside their own borderline reality. Sagittarius and Aquarius together want to break the rules and challenge the established. Uniqueness and nonconformity are such strong forces behind this relationship that it is difficult to establish an identity as a couple.*

***Sagittarius and Pisces**, these signs are the ultimate expression of their element in astrology. Sagittarius is* *a rustic fire and Pisces is an abyss in the sea. Because both signs are so expansive, neither can totally devour the other. Sagittarius will live contentedly by the vivid fantasy of Pisces, while Pisces will be suggestible by the adventurous soul of Sagittarius. Both signs are globetrotters, so it may be difficult to anchor this relationship. However, if both are content to keep the relationship in a less defined and more subtle realm, they will thrive as a fantastic couple.*

Sagittarius and Vocation

Sagittarius has a jovial spirit. They are the person to whom curious things happen, so they always have a story to tell.

They value their own and others' time. For this reason, they devote their attention only to people they feel they can learn something from.

It is inspiring and makes others feel on top of the world. They help generously.

Best Professions

Sagittarius is famous for setting their sights on a purpose and achieving it. They strive to get what they want. Their belief system is immutable.

They have a natural enthusiasm and seek new experiences. Sagittarians cannot stand still and have a need to explore. Veterinarians, Theologians, Lawyers, Diplomats, and Travel Agents.

Signs not to do business with

Sagittarius is incompatible with Cancer and Scorpio, these two signs belonging to the emotional water element, and they need time to feel secure, something that Sagittarius does not admit in business.

Signs to be associated with

It is positively associated with Pisces, Libra, Capricorn, Cancer, and Leo. These signs have an innate ability for business.

Money Rituals

Spell to multiply Money.

You need:

- 1 bill of any value

- 1 silver or gold colored envelope

- 1 Pencil, ballpoint pen or green ink

This spell should be cast on a Thursday, if possible, at the time of the Sun, the planet Jupiter, or Mars.

On the bill you will write in green your full name, date, and place of birth on one side. On the other side you write: "Prosperity and abundance are present in my life". Place the bill inside the envelope and seal it. Fold the envelope in half and place it under your bed at the level of your head. It should remain there for 10 days. After this period, you must spend the bill.

Wiccan Money Spell.

This spell is most effective during the solstices.

You should get a gold-colored ribbon that is approximately forty centimeters long. You take the ribbon by one end and tie nine knots.

As you tie each knot you must repeat aloud the following phrases: "I begin my spell with knot #1.

With knot #2 my work will be valuable.

With knot #3, the money comes to me.

With knot #4, abundance knocks on my door. With knot #5, my economy progresses.

With knot #6, this spell has worked.

With knot #7 I receive success in what I ask for.

With knot #8, fortune smiles on me.

With knot #9, everything I have asked for is fulfilled". The tape should be kept with you or in a place where you can watch it daily.

Spell of Abundance.

You need:

- 1 egg

- 1 piece of yellow paper

- 1 Pen

- Sacred water

Make a small hole in the egg and drain all the egg white and yolk. Clean the inside and outside of the egg with the holy water.

Next, take the small piece of paper and write down the amount of money you would like to receive.

Place the paper inside the egg.

You can decorate the outside with the symbol of money.

Bury the egg in your yard or in a potted plant.

In doing so, you say, "In this land all my money multiplies and grows."

Ritual to Get Money in Three Days.

Get five cinnamon sticks, a dried orange peel, a liter of Full Moon water and a silver candle. Boil the cinnamon and orange peel in the Moon water.

When it cools, place it in a spray bottle. Light the candle in the north part of the living room of your house and spray all rooms with the liquid. As you do this repeat in your mind: "Spirit Guides protect my home and let me receive the money I need immediately".

When you are finished, leave the candle burning.

Money with a White Elephant

Buy a white elephant with the trunk facing up. Place it facing the inside of your home or business, never facing the doors.

On the first day of each month, place a bill of the lowest value in the elephant's trunk, folded in two lengthwise and repeat: "May this be doubled by 100"; then fold it again widthwise and repeat: "May this be multiplied by a thousand".

Unfold the bill and leave it in the elephant's trunk until the following month. Repeat the ritual, changing the bill.

Lottery Winning Ritual.

You need:

- 2 green candles

- 12 coins (representing the twelve months of the year)

- 1 tangerine

- Cinnamon stick

- Petals of 2 red roses

-1 wide-mouthed glass jar with lid

-1 old lottery ticket

- Full Moon Water

In the jar place the tangerine, around it the lottery ticket, the coins, the petals, and the cinnamon, cover it with the Luna water and put the lid on it.

Place the candle on the lid of the jar and light it. The next day you will replace the candle with a new one and on the third day you will uncover the container, throw away everything except the coins, which will serve as an amulet.

Keep one in your wallet and leave the other eleven at home. At the end of the year, you must spend the coins.

Ritual to Improve Finances.

You need:

- 12 coins

- Mandarin oil

- 12 golden candles in pyramid shape

- 1 white plate

- 12 citrines

- Silver pouch

Place the lit candle in the center of the plate and the 12 coins around it forming a circle. Place the citrines next to the coins.

Scatter a few drops of tangerine oil around it. Keep a golden candle burning for 12 days. After this period, discard the candle remains. Place the citrines and coins in the silver bag and put it under your mattress at the head of your bed.

Ritual to always have Cash.

You need:

- 1 crystal glass

- 15 Coins

- 1 bill for current use

- 1 gold candle

- 1 new sewing needle

- 3 amethyst quartz

You must perform this ritual on a Friday at the time of the planet Venus or the Sun.

Place inside the cup the coins, the amethysts and the bill folded in four parts. Write with the needle in the candle the symbol of money ($$).

You light the candle and repeat in your mind: "Abundance surrounds me and I claim my share of what I get in this abundant universe".

You take the bill and hide it in your wallet.

The cup with the coins and the amethysts should be placed to the left of the door of your house.

Express Money Spell.

This spell is most effective if you cast it on a Thursday.

You are going to fill a glass bowl with rice. Then you light a green candle (which you must have previously consecrated) and place it in the center of the bowl.

You light the cinnamon incense and circle the fountain with its smoke clockwise six times.

While performing this procedure, mentally repeat: "I open my mind and heart to wealth.

Abundance comes to me, now and all is well.

The universe is radiating wealth into my life, now."

Leftovers can be disposed of in the trash.

Prosperity Potion.

In a saucepan put seven cinnamon sticks, seven basil leaves, chamomile, cloves, and Full Moon water. Boil it all for 10 minutes, when it reaches the boiling point remove it from the fire and cover it to cool down. Every day at 7:00 pm you will drink a cup of this preparation to which you will add honey to your liking. While you drink it repeat in your mind: "My wealth is already within me. I attract money and wonderful opportunities in abundance. Wealth is part of my existence."

Ritual to Win Money in Casinos.

You must get a green candle, a yellow candle, a white elephant (figure), a yellow sheet of paper and gold ink pen. You write on the sheet of paper the name of the casino.

Roll up the paper and put it in the elephant's trunk.

You place the green candle on the right side of the elephant and the yellow one on the left side, then you light them. This ritual is most effective on a Thursday at the time of the planet Jupiter or the Sun.

Ritual for Money with Santa Muerte

You need:

- 1 image of the golden Santa Muerte

- 7 coins in common use

- 1 magnet

- 1 white plate

- 1 red sachet

- 1 gold ribbon

- 1 gold candle

- 1 new sewing needle

You must write with the needle the word prosperity thirteen times on the golden candle.

Place this candle in front of the figure, which you must have previously placed on the white plate with the magnet and coins.

You light the candle and say this prayer to Santa Muerte: "Dear Death of my heart, do not forsake me of your protection, neither day nor night, my lady, I ask you to unblock my paths to success and fortune, that through this sacred flame all my supplications may reach you. Thank you, my lady, for having heard me". When the candle burns out, put the magnet and the coins in the red bag, tie it with the golden ribbon. You must carry it with you for thirteen days.

Then you take it to a cemetery and leave it there.

Best Countries and Cities to Live In

Countries: *Saudi Arabia, Australia, Chile, Hungary, Spain, South Africa, Ukraine, Madagascar, United States, Cuba, Mexico, El Salvador, Panama, Colombia, Portugal, and Brazil.*

Cities: *Moravia, Tuscany, Provence, Narbonne, Buda, Cologne, Nottingham, Sheffield, Stuttgart, Santiago de Chile, Santa Clara, and Toronto.*

Incense and Essential Oils for Money

Palo Santo Incense and Essential Oil. Its main benefit is spiritual cleansing, but it is perfect for use if you are in a period of negotiation or contract signing.

Plants for Money

Geranium: *is one of the oldest plants attributed with magical properties.*

It is used for love, fertility and for protection against witchcraft. Another advantage is that it will also attract money to your home.

Quartz for Money

Orange Calcite: it *is used to attract prosperity to the home and abundance. It is not only beneficial for finances, but also for creativity and self-improvement.*

Green Calcite is a powerful talisman to attract wealth to your business.

This stone vibrates with the energy of financial abundance in the universe.

Money Charms

The Pentacles of Jupiter that will guarantee you Prosperity.

Pentacles are magical figures, capable of transmitting positive energies to their environment. The action of Jupiter's pentacles derives from the combination of letters, signs, and beneficial formulas, they symbolize graphically and mystically a wish. They clearly act on the psyche of people who have visual contact with him.

The largest compilation of pentacles is found in The Clavicles of King Solomon, a volume of high magic attributed to this biblical king. In it are 36 pentacles that have various purposes and among them are the seven pentacles of Jupiter.

Pentacles to Thrive.

The purpose of these pentacles is to provide abundance, resolve work-related conflicts, and to assist with

more directly perceive all kinds of benefits that grant greater prosperity.

Jupiter, the so-called Great Benefic in astrology, is a planet that is related to expansion, optimism, links with powerful people and the ability to make fortune. You should draw them with great concentration and with the intention that they manifest your will. The most suitable material is a piece of parchment. Once finished, they should be hung somewhere that is visible such as the cash register or in your wallet (you can print them).

Affirmations to Receive Money

You should perform these decrees for 21 days so that you can see the results, if possible three times a day. If you repeat them aloud, they will be more powerful.

I am perfect abundance and divine wealth.

- *I am prosperity in my business and finances.*

- *I am the divine wisdom that intelligently shapes all existence. I walk safely through abundance. I see myself in prosperity.*

- *I have the power to create my own world. My dreams materialize because I persevere in them. Everything I set my mind to; I achieve it.*

Vacations

Vacations provide physical and mental benefits. It has been proven that vacationing lowers stress levels and benefits the immune system. Sometimes planning a vacation causes stress because there are infinite options and deciding becomes a chimerical task.

Using astrology, understanding your personality provides insight into the ideal vacation spot for you.

***Aries**, an all-inclusive resort with outdoor sports activities in a warm location such as Punta Cana, Cancun and the Turks and Caicos Islands would be ideal. Australia is an exciting country that offers a wealth of emotions to make your heart race.*

***Taurus**, a stay in a luxurious resort on Cayman Island, or a luxurious vacation in Dubai, in a hotel that has all the amenities will be very appealing. Italy is a perfect country because there you will find everything you have always dreamed of love, charm, luxury, wonderful food, and first-class wines.*

***Gemini** loves to feel intellectually engaged. Travel with guided excursions such as a safari in Africa or researching the species of the Galapagos Islands offer the zodiac communicator a luxurious experience.*

Cancer, *short trips, surrounded by family and friends. Disney World, enjoying the attractions and its diverse foods is one option. In Orlando, Florida, there are multiple fantastic hotels and resorts, each with a unique and fascinating theme.*

Leo, *staying in a bungalow over the sea in Tahiti is fantastic for this sign. Another luxury alternative, something the lion loves, would be to rent a private tropical island in the Maldives, Fiji, or the Virgin Islands.*

Virgo, *Italy is your best option. This country will keep you well occupied. As an earth sign you connect with the world around you, places like La Romana in the Dominican Republic, Puerto Viejo in Costa Rica, and Belo Horizonte in Brazil will inject life into you.*

Libra, *go for cities with museums. Tropical vacations will not be as satisfying for Libra as touring the Louvre in Paris, the Acropolis Museum in Athens, Greece, the Prado Museum in Madrid, Spain or the Uffizi Gallery in Florence, Italy.*

Scorpion, *spend a few days on a secluded beach with liquor and massages. In Greece, Bali, St. Martin, or Hawaii you will find all these luxuries. Visiting heritage sites near your luxury hotel would be an extraordinary combination of tropical and cultural vacation. Mykonos and Roda in Greece are perfect destinations.*

Sagittarius, *explore the Camino de Santiago, a network of quite different paths, all leading to the city of Santiago de Compostela. Each path has its history, heritage, and magic. Sagittarius is a traveler who craves new experiences so in Ireland you will find everything you are looking for.*

Capricorn, *a purposeful sign. Vacations where you can make new business relationships. China would be spectacular. Capricorn has a sense of historical value that other signs do not have, so countries like Israel and Egypt where history is present will make you feel at home.*

Aquarius *loves innovative ideas, unknown places, and new relationships. A fantastic country to visit would be Japan not only for its fascinating history and* *culture, but because each of its regions has something different to offer.*

Pisces*, a water sign that is happy with tropical vacations. A beachfront hotel would be ideal. The island "La Dique" in the Republic of Seychelles, the most beautiful beach in the world will be a sure success. Pisces, possessing a calm outlook on life, being ruled by Neptune makes you a creative thinker. Sweden is a country he should visit because there he will find a culture as innovative as he is.*

Who is your soul mate according to your zodiac sign?

When we hear the term "soul mates," we usually think of them as referring to members of a couple, i.e., someone with whom you have a strong sentimental-sexual connection. However, legitimate soul mates do not always relate to each other from that point of view, and often are not even interested in the sexual aspect of a relationship.

Your soul mate may not only be your partner, but also your parent, friend, child, grandparent, boss, or sister.

From an astrological point of view and considering that the lessons we need to learn before reaching the next spiritual level are the ones that define the type of affective relationships, we need to develop in life today, we can say that Cancer and Pisces are soul mates of Aries.

With Cancer and Pisces, Aries can not only focus better and resolve conflicts without violence, but also develop empathy, that is, the ability to put themselves in the other's place and learn to share.

These two signs do not like conflicts, and if they do arise, they prefer dialogue to any episode of brutality.

Aries can teach Cancer and Pisces not to need the approval of others, to be more risk-taking, and not to try to please everyone, i.e., to be more assertive.

The sensual Taurus, enemy of change, inbred relative of inertia, has as his soul mate Sagittarius and Gemini, two signs that know that life is a fascinating journey, but not a static one.

They can teach Taurus that it does not have to stay where it no longer must be for fear of uncertainty, and that there will always be certain situations or circumstances that will happen without us expecting them, and without us possessing any power to modify them. Taurus also has a lot to teach these signs.

Lessons of willpower, to have commitments with others, to be committed to what they do and to continue to the end with persistence, without haste or slowness. To have principles, and to be prudent.

Leo can balance a lot of karma with their soul mates belonging to Libra and Aquarius.

A Leo may become obstinate with a wrong idea or belief out of vanity; Libra and Aquarius know that behind an egocentric person there is a low self-esteem.

Libra will teach Leo equanimity and tolerance, to use reasoning and diplomacy to maintain smooth communication. Aquarius, the opposite sign to Leo, equipped with objective and fair judgment as they are never swayed by prejudice, will teach Leo to see people's hearts, to offer their shoulder and give sympathetic words in times of need.

Leo never hesitates when making decisions, and if they do, they do not manifest it, something that Libra should practice.

Fidelity is a hallmark in Leo, something unknown to Aquarius, and the little lions can give him moral lessons.

Virgo, known as perfectionists because of their immense fear of failure, has Scorpio and Capricorn as soul mates. Virgo likes to be rigorous in their decisions and has a prototype in every aspect of their life. This selectivity holds them back from following the movement of life.

Virgo will tear an entire project apart if they feel it was not perfect in the first place, something a Capricorn would never do as their vision will allow them to see that alternative measures can always be taken, without having to start over.

Capricorn is a sign sure of their own space, they do not make meaningless decisions, something Virgo sometimes does.

On the other hand, Scorpio can mitigate the worst and enhance the best of Virgo. Scorpio and Virgo have a practical approach to life; however, Scorpio is much more of a life-lover than Virgo. Scorpio will bring the decisiveness that Virgo lacks, and Virgo will bring control and rationality to the enthusiastic Scorpio.

Virgo will make Capricorn more pleasant and playful at his side, isolating him from that excessive seriousness that he often shows in his face.

Madness and Zodiac Signs

Madness has been revealed throughout history as an obscure, enigmatic, and conflicting truth. It has frightened us, we have ignored it and even accepted it, and as a result, the people who have suffered from it have been rejected, eliminated, and honored.

Any behavior that is incongruent with our reasoning is not necessarily an act of insanity, but a unique way of proceeding.

It is a mistake if, when we feel affected or annoyed by the actions or follies of others, we banish them, since this does not make us more reasonable, balanced, or perfect, but rather makes us just as crazy.

Defining insanity is as complex as defining sanity, but all zodiac signs have their degree of insanity.

Cancer*: They are temperamental. This causes them to have an incomprehensible personality seen from the outside. The popularity of crazy people was earned by their inconsistent character that sometimes disturbs the people around them.*

Scorpio: *They need change to be happy, they can do crazy things just to generate some action. For them* *having an outburst is normal because they are addicted to change and frenzies.*

Pisces: *It is impossible for them not to infect you with their madness. Their instability and imbalance bother the people around them. They see everything as rosy, which makes them be called crazy because they are always floating on a cloud.*

Gemini: *He is famous for his duality. They are sometimes in conflict with themselves. They love challenges that involve danger. They love to plan impromptu adventures and are always ready to border the limits of maximum madness.*

Leo: *When the fire settles in their head, they think that everything that surrounds their life is more urgent than anything else. They are extravagant and have attitudes that for others are considered crazy. They can do things that a reasonable person would never do.*

Aries: *They upset themselves and anyone around them. They are stubborn and like to be the first in everything, even if for that they must commit crazy* *things. They do not know how to retract, something that leads them to perform irrational acts.*

Aquarius: *A rebellious and free sign, which does not care in the least about the opinion they have of them. It acts in a capricious way, with crazy attitudes that break the paradigms.*

Sagittarius: *He is fun, but violent with his desire for action. They do not know how to measure the consequences of their actions, something that many consider madness. It is not strange to see them totally unbridled, crossing the terrain of irresponsibility.*

Libra: *They long for happiness and harmony, and to get it they are willing to do anything crazy. They are unstable, and that leads them to break their commitments, something that many consider crazy.*

Virgo: *They go to extremes and become obsessive. They have a vision of what they want written in stone, no one can give them advice, they do not let themselves be guided. When they do not listen, they commit various follies.*

Taurus*: When an idea lands in their mind there is no one to banish it, even committing crazy things to corroborate their hypothesis. Try to evaluate their patience and you will discover how far their level of madness goes.*

Capricorn*: He forgets absolutely nothing, does not forgive and much less, forgets, if you do something wrong, do not worry because he will remind you for a lifetime to drive you completely crazy. Capricorn is insanely obsessive about control.*

The psychology behind the lottery.

Lottery games are extremely popular all over the world.

We all have the impossible dream of winning the lottery, since the illusion of being millionaires, by a stroke of luck, even if the odds are minimal, is the main reason people play.

Players perceive that the cost of the lottery ticket, in relation to the profits they would obtain if they won, is minuscule. We always perceive risk emotionally, and if it causes us pleasure, we tend to see the risk as insignificant and neutralize the emotion of danger, focusing only on the benefits.

Players see the lottery as a unique opportunity to be rewarded by investing little money, and with little exposure to risk.

Games have both traditional and superstitious aspects. Some people always play the same numbers because they are their favorites, relate them to a significant date, or have dreamed them.

Others play at a specific time, day, or place. When we think we are in control, we feel confident, because when we choose the numbers ourselves, instead of playing at random, although the chances of being right are the same, we have the impression that we are controlling destiny, and that the chances are in our favor.

There are people who only play for fun, in these cases the lottery transcends the economic cost, becoming a fun that is enlivened when they conjecture everything, they can do with the money they would acquire.

There are five psychological descriptions of individual lottery players:

The adventurer, *who is bewitched by games involving large sums of money, speculating with random numbers, and with planned numbers.*

The competitor, *who insists on showing off through gambling that he bets to win.*

The greedy, *who has no boundaries for gambling, and is not afraid to take risks when betting.*

The tactician, *never playing risky, looks for tactics, strategies, and numerical sets when playing the numbers.*

The superstitious person, *who always plays the same number combinations, uses talismans, rituals, or will buy his tickets on a specific date and place.*

Is there a trick or formula to win the lottery?

That question is still unanswered. There are many who speculate, and claim, that you are more likely to be struck by lightning before you win the lottery. Although others study the odds with great perseverance and subtlety.

Playing the lottery, or any other game of chance if it is done with measure, is a cheap way to buy illusions and confidence in the future. The complication arises when the person does not control his impulses to play, generating an addiction to gambling and falling into compulsive gambling.

A gambling addict is an individual to whom gambling causes great difficulties at work and in his family relationships, since losses induce him to gamble larger amounts of money with the aspiration of recovering the lost money. This becomes a vicious circle, and the only way to solve it is with psychotherapeutic treatment.

The best gifts for zodiac signs

Gift giving is a universal way to show that we care and appreciate a person, but gift buying can be a challenge, for some a real headache.

The planets can help you once, knowing the zodiac sign of the person, you may be able to make the ideal gift.

***Fire signs: Aries, Leo and Sagittarius** like gifts that make them feel important, related to sports, travel, and technology.*

A professional digital camera, the latest model of iPhone, a plane ticket with hotel included to an exotic tourist spot or with historical background, business books, sportswear or exercise equipment, lottery tickets, bottles of fine wine and exclusive branded shoes will please these signs.

***Taurus, Virgo and Capricorn**, who belong to the earth element, are sometimes traditional, but that does not mean they do not like gifts from recognized brands.*

A painting of a famous painter, a belt or briefcase to carry their work papers, a wallet with their initials, branded perfumes, massages or body treatments, a pet, bathrobes, cozy pajamas, or even aromatherapy diffusers will make them happy.

***Air signs: Gemini, Libra and Aquarius** are not materialistic, and the functionality of a gift is much more important than the price. Their imagination is abundant, and anything that stimulates this capacity appeals to them.*

A cell phone, computer or IPad, books on personal growth, spirituality, philosophy and alternative therapies, self-help and economic empowerment courses, a telescope, tickets to the opera or theater, an animal that does not have to be caged, quartz, essential oils, incense, and after-bath colognes will be highly appreciated by these signs.

***Cancer, Scorpio and Pisces**, the water signs, will love personalized gifts. Cooking utensils, a romantic dinner on the beach under the moonlight, a relaxing massage in a spa, daring lingerie, slippers or a comfortable sofa to watch TV, a bottle of champagne, scented candles, amulets, astrology books, a set of tarot cards, lotions, perfumes and beauty accessories, wine, cookies, preserves and all variety of gourmet products are on the list of gifts that these signs will accept with great pleasure.*

Giving gifts is a blessing, it is a gesture of generosity; giving gifts is a symbolic act that represents a compliment, an attention to someone we want to please and symbolizes the affection we profess.

When we give gifts, relationships are improved and strengthened, and joy is generated.

The zodiac signs and their fears.

The twelve signs of the zodiac symbolize twelve essential archetypes of the human personality, but at the same time they are psychological prototypes, which is why each of the zodiac signs has a specific and personal fear.

Let us remember that fear is an essential human alarm and defense mechanism. It only becomes a problem when it is excessive.

*Fears are insecurities and sometimes we project them with the opposite actions as it is the case of the **Aries** sign; recognized for their iron will, nothing and nobody paralyzes them. They love to control everything, and their most ingrained fear is to fail or ask for help, because for them this is synonymous of weakness.*

***Taurus** is the most stubborn of the earth signs. Change terrifies them, as well as running out of money, they spend their lives saving because poverty frightens them.*

***Gemini**, the communicator of the zodiac, a bit anxious and insecure, they try to attract attention because they dread looking boring. Legitimate children of the*

Moon, Cancers love their safety zone because no one can hurt them there, they are terrified of loneliness and rejection.

***Leo**, the king of the zodiac, leaders and brave, were not born to lose. Their most ingrained fear is to go unnoticed; they prefer to be spoken ill of, but not to be ignored.*

*The master of neatness **Virgo** sometimes becomes compulsive about health, so they are hypochondriacs. Their main fear is getting sick, but disorganization scares them more than anything else.*

*Exceptionally intelligent **Libra** are indecisive and therein lies their primary fear: making decisions. Another of their fears is loneliness.*

*Enigmatic and seductive **Scorpios** have an elephant's memory, they fear betrayal and if you do something they dislike, they will keep it from you forever. Never keep a secret from a Scorpio.*

*The adventurer of the zodiac, **Sagittarius** panics about commitment because the demands are terrifying. They* *are very funny, but behind that smile hides the fear of being deceived.*

*Demanding to the extreme, **Capricorns** never stray from their goals; their main fear is to make mistakes, especially at the professional level. They are self-sacrificing and fear not achieving their dreams.*

*The rebellious and utopian **Aquarius** fear losing their freedom, this would mean losing their own essence. They always have many friendships, but none of them bind them. They need the group, but do not want the group to need them.*

*Peace is synonymous with **Pisces**, they hate confrontations. Compassionate to the core, they are afraid to see others suffer. They are a little insecure, have stage fright and fear rejection.*

Some old astrology books hold Saturn responsible for fear in a natal chart, I think that for fear to originate, the alliance of several planets with their corresponding energies must manifest.

That is, fears are represented by various planets linked by aspects, there is no specific planet that is necessarily related to the development of any type of fear.

Moon in Sagittarius

If you have the Moon in Sagittarius, you like to feel free to explore and expand your horizons. You are enthusiastic, and you like to share your feelings.

You like to feel active, and interact with other people, cultures, and philosophies. You are always up for an adventure, and open to learning new things.

The smallest lie is a big problem for you, because the search for truth is essential to feel safe. You can forgive anything except lies and betrayal.

You need to feel that you have enough freedom to explore your own path and discover your own truth.

When you feel threatened, your immediate reaction is to escape. If you are unhappy, or do not feel safe, in a situation, you will leave.

Your freedom and your truth are the most essential aspects of your security. The moment either is missing, you will want to leave the situation, or leave a relationship.

They never allow difficulties to disappoint them, because, even if the past or the present is dark, they always hope for a better future.

They hate routine or experiencing problems all the time, they need an escape valve.

They are romantic in relationships; however, their emotional side does not enjoy jealousy.

They crave strong emotions.

People born with the Moon in Sagittarius are optimistic by nature. They have blind confidence in the future, and this allows them to take risks, something that can be both good and bad at the same time.

They are people with a strong need for freedom, who become overwhelmed if they feel tied down.

They are very dedicated to themselves, but they are not selfish.

The importance of the Ascendant Sign

The Sun sign has a major impact on who we are, but the Ascendant is what really defines us, and that could even be the reason you do not identify with some traits of your zodiac sign.

Really the energy that your sun sign gives you makes you feel different from the rest of the people, for that reason, when you read your horoscope sometimes you feel identified and gives sense to some predictions, and that happens because it helps you to understand how you could feel and what will happen to you, but it only shows you a percentage of what could really be.

The Ascendant is different from the Sun sign because it reflects who we are superficially, that is, how others see you or the energy you transmit to people, and this is so real that you may meet someone and if you predict their sign, you may have discovered their Ascendant sign and not their Sun sign.

 In summary, the characteristics you see in someone when you first meet them is the Ascendant, but since our lives are affected, we relate to others, the Ascendant has a major impact on our daily lives.

It is a bit complex to explain how the Ascendant sign is calculated or determined, because it is not the position of a planet that determines it, but the sign that was rising on the eastern horizon at the time of your birth, as opposed to your sun sign, which depends on the precise time you were born.

Thanks to technology and the Universe today is easier than ever to know this information, of course if you know your birth time, or if you have an idea of the time but there is not a margin of more than hours, because there are many websites that make the calculation by entering the data, astro.com is one of them, but there is infinite.

This way, when you read your horoscope you can also read your Ascendant and know more personalized details, you will see that from now on if you do this your way of reading the horoscope will change and you will know why that Sagittarius is so modest and pessimistic if in fact they are so exaggerated and optimistic, and this is perhaps because he has a Capricorn Ascendant, or because that Scorpio colleague is always talking about everything, no doubt he has a Gemini Ascendant.

I am going to synthesize the characteristics of the different Ascendants, but this is also very general since these characteristics are modified by planets in conjunction with the Ascendant, planets aspecting the Ascendant, and the position of the ruler planet of the sign in the Ascendant.

For example, a person with an Aries Ascendant with its ruling planet, Mars, in Sagittarius will respond to the environment a little differently than another person, also with an Aries Ascendant, but whose Mars is in Scorpio.

Similarly, a person with a Pisces Ascendant who has Saturn conjunct him will "behave" differently than someone with a Pisces Ascendant who does not have that aspect.

All these factors modify the Ascendant, astrology is overly complex, and horoscopes are not read or made with tarot cards, because astrology is not only an art but also a science.

It can be common to confuse these two practices, and this is because, although they are two different concepts, they have some points in common. One of these common points is based on their origin and is that both procedures have been known since ancient times.

They are also similar in the symbols they use, since both present ambiguous symbols that need to be interpreted, requiring specialized reading and training to know how to interpret these symbols.

There are thousands of differences, but one of the main ones is that while in tarot the symbols are perfectly understandable at first glance, being figurative cards, although it is necessary to know how to interpret them well, in astrology we observe an abstract system which is necessary to know previously to interpret them, and of course it must be said that, although we can recognize the tarot cards, anyone can not interpret them correctly.

Interpretation is also a difference between the two disciplines because while tarot does not have an exact time reference, since the cards are placed in time only thanks to the questions asked in the corresponding spread, astrology does refer to a specific position of the planets in history, and the interpretation systems used by both are diametrically opposed.

The astrological chart is the basis of astrology, and the most important aspect to make the prediction. The astrological chart must be perfectly elaborated for the reading to be successful and to learn more about the person.

To draw up a birth chart, it is necessary to know all the data about the birth of the person in question.

It must be known exactly, from the exact time it was delivered, to the place where it was done.

The position of the planets at the time of birth will reveal to the astrologer the points he needs to draw up the birth chart.

Astrology is not only about knowing your future, but also about knowing the important points of your existence, both present and past, to make better decisions to decide your future.

Astrology will help you to know yourself better, so that you can change the things that block you or enhance your qualities.

And if the astrological chart is the basis of astrology, the tarot reading is fundamental in the latter discipline. Like who makes you the astrological chart, the seer who makes you the tarot spread, will be the key to the success of your reading, so it is best to ask for tarot readers recommended, and although surely you cannot answer specifically to all the questions you ask yourself in your life, a correct reading of the tarot spread, and the cards that come out in the roll, will help guide you about the decisions you make in your life.

In summary, astrology, and tarot use symbolism, but the main question is how all this symbolism is interpreted.

truly a person who masters both techniques will undoubtedly be an immense help to the people who will ask for advice.

Many astrologers combine both disciplines, and regular practice has taught me that both usually flow very well, providing an enriching component in all prediction issues, but they are not the same and you cannot do a horoscope with tarot cards, nor can you do a tarot reading with an astrological chart.

Ascendant in Sagittarius

People with an Ascendant in Sagittarius have noble ideals and lofty goals.

This Ascendant is synonymous with exploration, travel, and optimism. People with this Ascendant see life as a journey and enjoy the road and what emerges as the fruit of destiny.

These people need to have goals and objectives to feel fulfilled. The way they live their lives inspires others around them.

These people must be careful because they can perish in the face of exaggeration and exuberance, living beyond their means.

Aries - Sagittarius Ascendant

Aries with Sagittarius Ascendant are energetic people, who do not let themselves be frightened by anything and who have a lot of self-confidence. They always have a smile on their lips.

In the professional area, they tend to be leaders and tend to excel in professions that require initiative. They have enthusiasm and optimism, making them not only initiative but also love to keep growing.

Professionally, they tend to do well in positions that require an open mind and leadership skills.

In romantic relationships it is likely to be easy for them to find a partner and for this to last for a long time, although an affair is likely to arise along the way.

Sometimes they are selfish and irresponsible with their actions. They can get carried away by passion and risk doing dangerous things.

Taurus - Sagittarius Ascendant

Taurus Ascendant Sagittarius is characterized by its generosity and positivity in life.

Professionally, these people are diligent workers, known for their perseverance and effort. They only rest when they complete their goals, which are always impeccably accomplished due to their demand and pursuit of perfection.

Emotionally, they value simplicity in love relationships and excel in sensuality and passion. When these people are in love, they do everything possible to maintain their loyalty and fulfill their commitment to their partner.

These people are prone to work beyond what is healthy, disregarding their own limits and hours of rest.

Gemini - Sagittarius Ascendant

Gemini Ascendant Sagittarius is a harmonious combination. For these people it is essential to be accompanied by someone sympathetic, who offers a pleasant and uncritical dialogue.

Despite the variations in their moods, they do their best to keep life interesting and away from boredom.

In professional terms, their nature is versatile and adaptable, allowing them to take on multiple roles at once. Gemini with Sagittarius Ascendant often struggle to find lasting satisfaction and fulfillment, resulting in frequent job changes.

In love relationships, passion is not the primary factor; what is essential for them is to establish a healthy and fraternal camaraderie that allows for a more solid and lasting bond.

These people tend to have ephemeral and superficial relationships. Their constant search for companionship and their innate inclination toward enthusiastic experiences can lead to unsatisfactory relationships.

Cancer - Sagittarius Ascendant

Cancer Ascendant Sagittarius are extroverted people, and skilled in social relationships. Sagittarius.

Professionally, these people are accompanied by fortune, and this has a direct impact on their financial life. They are always involved in multiple business projects and activities.

In love relationships, they experience a series of intense loves. The influence of Sagittarius lessens Cancer's preoccupation with the stability of relationships, focusing more on the present. Their relationships tend to be quite sensual, and they place a high value on sexuality.

Leo - Sagittarius Ascendant

Leo Ascendant Sagittarius are bold and often have a natural desire to immerse themselves in intense and meaningful experiences. They are drawn to a variety of interests, although their passion is inclined toward exploration and long journeys. They have an innate drive to set and pursue important goals and objectives.

In the work field, they usually stand out for their determination and ambition. When they find a project that excites them, they stick with it to completion, not allowing obstacles to deter them. They have a remarkable determination to succeed and a natural talent for business.

Emotionally, their optimistic and cheerful attitude has a contagious effect on their environment. They are endowed with a remarkable capacity for seduction.

They enjoy love and fleeting relationships but have trouble making lasting commitments.

Virgo - Sagittarius Ascendant

Virgo Sagittarius Ascendants possess the intellectual capacity to achieve wonderful things in life. However, their propensity for change causes them to easily alter the course of their purpose, deviating from their desired goals.

In the work environment, their ambition and desire for self-knowledge lead them to achieve remarkable prestige. Sometimes, due to their indecision and diversification of interests, they do not achieve their goals.

Emotionally, these people have an intense sensuality exposing their innermost and deepest desires. When they find a partner who understands their complex personality, they reveal a wild side of themselves that is, on the one hand, cautious, and on the other, independent.

Libra - Sagittarius Ascendant

Libra with Sagittarius Ascendant are extraordinarily sociable people.

These people thrive in any job that gives them creative freedom and opportunities to interact with others.

When falling in love, Libra's innate tendency toward harmony is intensified by an extra dose of optimism. These people deeply appreciate the relationship and can honor the partner.

Libra Ascendant Sagittarius tend to rush into emotional decisions. This often results in early commitments and romantic failures.

Scorpio - Sagittarius Ascendant

Scorpio Ascendant Sagittarius look more approachable than they really are, creating a paradox inherent in this combination. They tend to need a certain degree of isolation to feel secure, and often project an extroverted personality.

In their work life they are more motivated in jobs that require research. They are helpful and fulfill to perfection everything that is entrusted to them.

Emotionally they have a powerful magnetism over those around them, they are usually extremely attractive people.

Sometimes they are inclined to seek control, interfere, and direct the course of others' lives.

Sagittarius - Sagittarius Ascendant

This combination reinforces the typical Sagittarius characteristics, their optimism and confidence stand out. They are very direct with their words, can sometimes offend others, and always try to draw a lesson from everything that happens to them in life.

In their work, they aim high with the goals they set for themselves because they love to challenge themselves. If they like what they do, they do not hesitate to give it their all.

In feelings they are people with low self-esteem, in need of external reinforcement to tell them that they are worth. They are honest people who will always function as they are, without masks.

Capricorn - Sagittarius Ascendant

Capricorns with Sagittarius Ascendant are demanding and meticulous.

Professionally they possess an objective perspective of their abilities. They are ambitious and persevering.

They take their relationships very seriously and consider themselves attractive and conquering people.

These people fluctuate between the excessive grandiosity of Sagittarius and the restrictions imposed by Capricorn. Sometimes their greed is not only limited to the financial aspect, but they may also lack ethical values.

Aquarius - Sagittarius Ascendant

Aquarius with Sagittarius Ascendant are people of great mental agility and are in constant search of knowledge. They are very communicative and empathetic.

At work they excel at completing large projects. They love to expand their horizons and take everything to the next level.

In their relationships, they are attracted to the unknown and the new, which makes it difficult for them to stay tied down in a relationship.

These people can become very impatient and take on too many things without finishing any of them.

Pisces - Sagittarius Ascendant

Pisces with Sagittarius Ascendant are very dedicated to their family, they love to protect. They are overly sensitive, intuitive, and responsible.

They can have difficulties to establish lasting affective bonds since they are always in search of new ones without being able to consolidate the old ones. It is complicated for them to have a stable partner.

They are very emotional and can lose their heads at any given moment. They find it difficult to make complicated decisions.

Saturn in Pisces, one of the most important astrological events.

March 7, 2023, was one of the most important days in that year's astrological calendar. Saturn, the stern teacher, and lord of karma, clashed with Pisces, the dreamer. This transit of Saturn in Pisces, which will last until February 2026, has not been a welcome mix.

Saturn is a planet of responsibility and strict authority, disciplining and structuring us as it transits through the zodiac. Saturn wants to make sure how we are achieving our goals, and when this planet moves through Pisces, the most spiritual sign, some important proposals are headed our way.

Pluto and Saturn, shifting in such unison, will bring a gigantic energetic volcano, and guaranteed to be an unforgettable period. This may sound like a formula for battle, but this energetic combo can be effective and profitable.

Saturn is not satisfied in Pisces. It is difficult for him to found structures and build reality when everything is shifting. Pisces is a dual sign, so it can express itself in opposite ways; it can be both transcendental and practical. There is the possibility that Saturn in Pisces indicates the construction of forms above or below the water, or to dominate the water, such as pipelines, aqueducts, and ports. But it can also reveal the collapse of these structures due to hurricanes or structural fragility.

The Pisces archetype is contradictory to Saturn. It represents utopia, creativity, spirituality, and esotericism, as well as dreams, illusions, lies and escapism. It symbolizes the aspiration to flow like the sea, breaking down boundaries and restrictions.

The last transit of Saturn in Pisces was from May 1993 to April 1996, this stage saw the results of the collapse of the Soviet Union in 1989 which caused after-effects all over the world and crushed the Russian economy. Russia waged the first Chechen war in 1994 which lasted until 1996.

The International Criminal Tribunal for the former Yugoslavia was established in The Hague in May 1993 to prosecute war crimes committed during the Yugoslav belligerents in the early 1990s.

On the other hand, the Bosnian war between Croats, Bosnians and Serbs spread with cruelties and ethnic cleansing, and various executions. The war ended in 1995, and most of the Bosnian Serb commanders were convicted of genocide and crimes against humanity. In 1994 the Rwandan genocide began when Hutu gangs murdered more than 700,000 Tutsis, and untold numbers of women were raped during the massacre, which finally ended in July. The Iraq disarmament crisis, after the end of the first Gulf War, was raging with a lot of noise and no trust among those involved. A sect in Switzerland called the "Order of the Solar Temple" conducted a string of crimes and mass suicides, and here in the United States, Timothy McVeigh murdered 168 people in the Oklahoma City bombing.

It was during this transit of Saturn through Pisces that O.J. Simpson was arrested for the murder of his ex-wife and boyfriend, and released after a lengthy trial that was quite a Hollywood-style spectacle.

In London, Fred West and his wife Rose were jailed after extractions in their backyard of the bodies of multiple murder victims.

South Africa had its first multiracial elections, and Nelson Mandela was elected president, later abolishing the death penalty in that country. Russia and China signed an agreement to stop provoking each other with their nuclear devices, and the Nuclear Non-Proliferation Treaty was endlessly amplified by 170 countries. In Australia, it was agreed to compensate indigenous people who were evicted during nuclear tests in the 1950s and 1960s.

Other events during the transit of Saturn in Pisces include religious currents, ideological movements such as socialism and leftism, the transmission of diseases and contagions, destructive behaviors induced by panic, an increase in the use of drugs and development of all types of art, as well as the means of maritime transportation.

Saturn in Pisces will see to it that we cannot use spirituality or fear to avoid certain conflicts that we must face. We can meditate, go to spend a hundred years in Tibet, and use the most powerful mantras in the universe, but at some point, we must also act.

During the last few years that Saturn has transited Aquarius, there has been a need to focus on individuality and being more genuine, rather than tolerating coercion from those around us. Although Aquarius is a sign known for dancing to its own beat, as Saturn is all about limitations, it has pushed us to sit alone with ourselves (remember the restrictions during the pandemic) and look at where we can place ourselves to create healthy boundaries.

All those lessons prepared us for what lies ahead with Saturn in Pisces. We will begin to be more sensible about how to add spirituality into our daily lives, while retaining an understanding of how to structure ourselves. Many people will abandon or question religions or dogmas.

Of course, there are many who will not savor this period, among them are religious guides and those who promote conspiracy theories. We will see conflicts between individuals of dissimilar religions, and many tendencies to try to dominate what others choose to believe.

We need to accept that just because others disagree with our beliefs, it does not mean they are wrong. It simply indicates that their views are different, because at the end of the day, Pisces stands for inclusiveness. Something we lack.

As Pisces and Neptune rule the entertainment business, major studios and record companies will close, and many artists who have been connected to those studios will decide to create their own. If you are an artist, it will be in your interest to use your work beneficially, rather than letting the big companies at the top enjoy the dividends.

There will be less interest in special effects and a greater orientation toward self-contained films and themes that reflect the everyday. We will appreciate the beauty around us and be less motivated by glamour.

Karma many times we tend to see it as something evil, but reaping what you sow is not bad if you have behaved well. Working with our karmic and subconscious baggage, understanding the past and being ready to let go, is decisive to manage this transit and come out of it successfully.

If you dodge this, Saturn will punish you, but if you embrace it, you will arrive at a place that is predestined for something great.

Saturn's placement in our natal chart indicates where we are compelled to gain control of reality and assume greater responsibility. Pisces is the last sign of the zodiac, so Saturn's movement here also indicates an end or completion point for a much larger cycle.

Pisces is a water sign representing light, darkness, and the invisible worlds. It is known for its abstract ideas, and creativity. Pisces is mutable, which means it is adaptable, and open to the energies of the world around it. Saturn is a very solid energy. It rules over law, responsibilities and restrictions, and its energy can sometimes feel like a wake-up call, bringing us back to reality and making us face the consequences of our actions.

Saturn's presence in Pisces could feel a bit heavy because of all this, as the normally watery, intuitive, and sensitive Piscean energy will be forced to become a bit more reserved.

To understand it better you can think of it this way: if Pisces is smooth flowing water, the presence of Saturn is going to build dams, and these holds can direct the water in a productive and beneficial direction, but it can also feel more oppressive or controlling. However, there is a way to create a balance between these two energies, as the creative, intangible, and external ideas of Piscean energy can get some roots thanks to Saturn.

Saturn has a practical energy, so, if we combine this with the creativity of Pisces, there is a balance that can be achieved to help us take our creative ideas and bring them to life or even turn them into a business.

Pisces is also connected to religion and spirituality, so with Saturn there could be many questions around religion and spirituality and how it is connected to the rules that govern society, the spiritual industry may also get a wake-up call under this energy, or on a personal level your own attitudes and beliefs about your spiritual or religious connection will change.

Really what Saturn wants us to do is to step up and take responsibility for our lives and act in accordance with our authentic selves. Saturn may impose limits and restrictions that make us feel trapped or stifled, but this is only so that we can take the time to discover what we really want and for what we are willing to stand.

Below, you can read a synthesis of what the transit of Saturn in Pisces will bring for each zodiac sign. If you want to get more out of all this information, I recommend that you read the one for your Ascendant sign, if you know it, and then mix the interpretations.

Another way to get more information about this powerful planetary transit is to think about the themes that developed in your life the last time Saturn was in Pisces, which was from 1994 to 1996, to get additional information about what this cycle can bring you.

How will it affect the Sagittarius Sign?

Saturn in Pisces is going to activate a divine corner of your birth chart. This corner will trigger issues related to who you are and who you present to the world. Are the two the same thing, or do you present a different version of yourself to the world? How deeply do you really know yourself?

We all wear masks, and we are all influenced by the opinions of others and the expectations of society. All of us alter our behavior when we are around certain people. While this is natural and normal, Saturn in Pisces will help you let go of the masks that no longer serve you.

This is a time to be real with yourself and who you really are.

No more pretending, no more hiding behind perfectionism, or running away to escape your problems. No more looking for that next adventure to distract you from the realities of your life.

You are going to be forced to be real with yourself, so that you can come home, so that you can connect with your roots and who you really are, away from all the masks and expectations that have been put on you. On this journey, you may very well return home or need to be close to your family. You may need to revisit your childhood wounds or discover that being close to your family triggers certain patterns within you.

Alternatively, the need to return home may also just be the need to return home within yourself, or to settle somewhere where you feel stable. There is this need to bring more stability into your life, to establish yourself in a kind of home.

Home is where the heart is, so it may very well apply here, but it would also not be surprising if certain factors arise for you around your home or your life.

Saturn energy in Pisces has a very stable feeling for you. If you have been looking to buy property, sell property or make home improvements, this energy can be very favorable. Of course, it is always important to follow your own instincts, but there is a strong focus around your home environment.

This energy can also be very favorable if you are looking to start a family or settle into a more committed relationship with someone. Saturn in Pisces is bringing roots into your life, and as you see those roots become integrated, it can help you know more clearly what you really want to be rooted to.

Sometimes, when we do not fully engage, even if unconsciously, we do not fully appreciate the consequences of what we are doing and by whom we are surrounded.

But with Saturn dangling some roots in front of us, the stakes become higher, and it becomes easier for us to realize what we want to be rooted to and what we do not want to be rooted to.

You may find the presence of these roots acting as a kind of awakening, helping you to realize what is meant for you and what you no longer wish to relate to.

Saturn is asking you what you want to be rooted to, and then will work to make sure you are taking responsibility for whatever roots you do.

Saturn in Pisces can bring a lot of weight and responsibility, but you decide what you want to give your energy to. Of course, sometimes life can get in the way and get in the way, but you can choose how you wish to spend your time. If you wish to stay grounded, under this energy, it may be necessary for you to move through a cycle of death and rebirth of some kind.

You may have to let go of some things, or some people.

You may have to put an end to behaviors or patterns that no longer serve you, and eventually you will be reborn, because you are stepping into a deeper and truer expression of who you are. It can be confronting to do this, and it can stir up a lot of fears and insecurities, when those masks come down, it can be difficult to navigate what we find underneath them, but you are beautiful or beautiful.

The real you, the unmasked you is perfect and exactly what is needed in the world right now.

Saturn will help you tear down the walls that have kept you trapped or hidden and guide you to build some new ones that allow you more openness and more freedom. As a fire sign, freedom is especially important to you, there is a stereotype for Sagittarius which is a horse in a field, the horse is happy in the field when the gate is left open because it can roam and play in the field.

But when the door is closed, the horse is unhappy, miserable and will do anything to escape.

While you are known as the free adventurer of the zodiac, Saturn is here to bring grounding into your life. Saturn may close the door, but it will open a window or another door you did not recognize before, giving you access to a whole new point of view. It can be triggering when Saturn in Pisces shows up, as it is a bit of a heavy energy and you are used to lightness, but there are deep lessons for you to learn and discover here.

There are many gifts that Saturn is waiting to impart. One of these gifts is simply a deeper and more connected understanding of who you are. Free from the masks and expectations of others and free from running away from your problems.

Saturn will make you confront them and sit with them until you have seen all they have to show you, but through this process, you will find even greater freedom.

You will be free of all that lurks in your shadows. You will be free of any shame or guilt or skeletons.

Saturn in Pisces may restrict you until you get there, but once you do the work, a whole new world will open for you, one that you will be even freer to explore.

Saturn is the guardian of our soul contract, this is the contract that our soul made before we entered this physical body, and Saturn wants to make sure that we are living according to it.

As you move through this Saturn in Pisces journey over the next few years, you will be aligning more closely with your soul contract.

You will feel more grounded to focus your energy on what really counts. While your home and family life may stand out, along with the masks you wear, at the end of the day, you are simply coming more into yourself.

You are being guided to detach from all that keeps you limited and small and move into the higher and deeper potential of your true self.

Bibliography

Some information was extracted from the books published by the authors: Love for all Hearts, Money for all Pockets and Horoscope 2022 and 2024.

Articles written in the Nuevo Herald by one of the writers.

About the Authors

In addition to her astrological knowledge, Alina Rubi has an abundant professional education; she holds certifications in Psychology, Hypnosis, Reiki, Bioenergetic Crystal Healing, Angelic Healing, Dream Interpretation and is a Spiritual Instructor. Rubi has knowledge of Gemology, which she uses to program stones or minerals and turn them into powerful Amulets or Talismans of protection.

Rubi has a practical and result-oriented character, which has allowed her to have a special and integrative vision of several worlds, facilitating solutions to specific problems. Alina writes the Monthly Horoscopes for the website of the American Association of Astrologers; you can read them at www.astrologers.com. At this moment she writes a weekly column in the newspaper El Nuevo Herald on spiritual topics, published every Sunday in digital form and on Mondays in print. He also has a program and weekly Horoscope on the YouTube channel of this newspaper. Her Astrological Yearbook is published every year in the newspaper "Diario las Américas", under the column Rubi Astrologa.

Rubi has authored several articles on astrology for the monthly publication "Today's Astrologer", has taught classes on Astrology, Tarot, Palm Reading, Crystal Healing, and Esotericism. She has weekly videos on esoteric topics on her YouTube channel: Rubi Astrologa. She had her own Astrology show broadcasted daily through Flamingo T.V., has been interviewed by several T.V. and radio programs, and every year she publishes her "Astrological Yearbook" with the horoscope sign by sign, and other interesting mystical topics.

She is the author of the books "Rice and Beans for the Soul" Part I, II, and III, a compilation of esoteric articles, published in English, Spanish, French, Italian and Portuguese. "Money for All Pockets", "Love for All Hearts", "Health for All Bodies", Astrological Yearbook 2021, Horoscope 2022, Rituals and Spells for Success in 2022, Spells and Secrets, Astrology Classes, Rituals and Charms 2024 and Chinese Horoscope 2024 are all available in five languages: English, Italian, French, Japanese and German.

Rubi speaks English and Spanish perfectly, combining all her talents and knowledge in her readings. She currently resides in Miami, Florida.

*For more information you can visit **the website** www.esoterismomagia.com*

Alina A. Rubi is the daughter of Alina Rubi. She is currently studying psychology at Florida International University.

Since she was a child, she has been interested in all metaphysical and esoteric subjects and has practiced astrology and Kabbalah since she was four years old. She has knowledge of Tarot, Reiki, and Gemology. She is not only the author, but also the editor, along with her sister Angeline A. Rubi, of all the books published by her and her mother.

*For more information, please contact her by email: **rubiediciones29@gmail.com***

www.ingramcontent.com/pod-product-compliance
Lightning Source LLC
Chambersburg PA
CBHW081220130726
47997CB00009B/2723